SPINNING WHEEL PRIMER

Alden Amos

First published by
Straw Into Gold
3006 San Pablo
Berkeley, California
1976

©Interweave Press, Inc., 1989
306 North Washington Avenue
Loveland, Colorado 80537

ISBN 0-934026-55-6

CONTENTS

ACKNOWLEDGMENTS

This booklet has been prepared by people who are themselves spinners. It is hoped that the information here contained is timely and useful. We invite your comment and suggestion.

Many people are involved in writing and producing a book (often the author is little more than a figurehead) and this work is no exception. To Susan Druding, Billy Bob, Bill Hersey, John Kyrk, the 'old' Straw staff, Bette and Bernie Hochberg, Linda Ligon and the Interweave Press folks . . . my heart-felt thanks. Last but not least, my special thanks for 'the wind beneath my wings', my chief squeeze and partner Stephenie Gaustad.

Alden Amos

INTRODUCTION

Spinning is a continuous process with you and your wheel in synchronized movement. It is important to learn what to expect of yourself as you spin. It is equally essential to know exactly what you can expect your wheel to do: how it moves; how the size and shape of various parts affect speed and the kinds of yarn for which it is best suited.

Although many books are available to teach you what you should be doing as you spin, this is the only book that tells you exactly how your wheel performs. It will show you how each type of wheel has its own strengths and weaknesses inherent in its design.

Since spinning is an interaction between you and your wheel, this information is very important to any serious spinner. It is necessary reading for anyone about to purchase a wheel.

The question and answer section gives easy, practical solutions to the problems every spinner will encounter.

Alden Amos is the most knowledgeable wheelmaker in the world today. You can trust his precise, authoritative information.

—Bette Hochberg

NAMING OF THE PARTS

1. maidens
2. bobbin
2a. bobbin whorl
3. flyer
3a. hooks
4. orifice
5. leather bearings
5a. bearing clearance adjustment screw
6. drive cord tension adjustment screw
7. mother-of-all
8. legs
9. treadle
10. treadle bar
11. treadle pivot supports
12. footman
12a. footman head
13. crank
14. drive wheel
15. drive cord
16. bench
17. wheel posts
18. bearing blocks

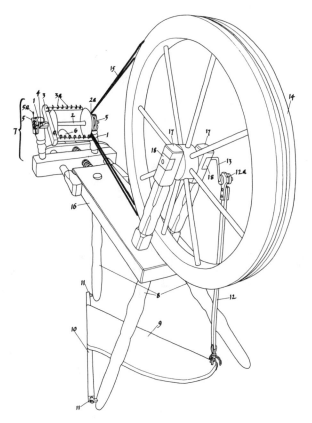

Typical Bobbin-lead Production Wheel

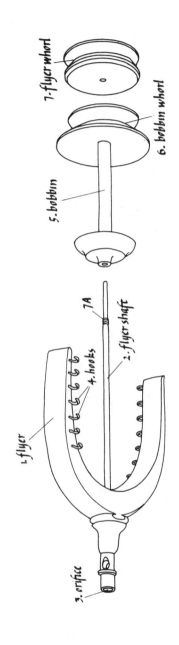

Figure 1. *Double-drive, bobbin-lead system.*

I. MECHANISMS

DOUBLE-DRIVE, BOBBIN-LEAD

Spinning wheels are fitted with one of several flyer - and - bobbin arrangements. Commonly encountered is the double-drive, bobbin-lead system, which will be used to illustrate the interaction of flyer and bobbin.

Figure 1 shows the components. The flyer (1) and flyer shaft (2) are assembled as a permanent unit, and include the orifice (3) and hooks (4). The bobbin (5) is fitted so that it is free to rotate on the flyer shaft. The bobbin whorl (6) is an integral part of the bobbin. The flyer whorl (7) is pressed or threaded onto the end (7-A) of the flyer shaft, in such a manner as to be locked in place. A practical system will allow the flyer whorl to be removed easily.

Figure 2 shows the assembled flyer and bobbin, mounted in operating position. Each strand of the doubled drive cord (8) is led over each whorl and around the driving wheel. As the drive wheel is turned, bobbin and flyer follow suit. Should both elements rotate at the same speed, spinning will take place; winding on, or the storing of the newly spun yarn, will not. It is necessary to rotate the elements at different speeds (with respect to each other) and this is done by making the bobbin whorl (6) smaller in diameter than the flyer whorl (7). The bobbin turns faster than the flyer, a situation referred to as bobbin-lead (pronounced leed).

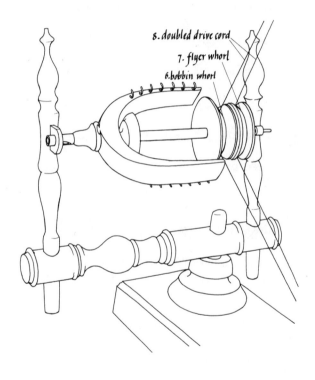

Figure 2. *Double-drive, bobbin-lead system assembled.*

The take-up, or wind-on rate, is determined by the differential speed of the two elements. The greater the difference in whorl diameter, the greater the lead, and the faster the wind-on rate. Different fibers (and weights of yarn) require different wind-on rates: A wheel set to spin a medium-weight wool yarn will need twice as much lead as a wheel set up to spin a medium-weight cotton, which requires more twist before wind-on.

SINGLE-DRIVE, FLYER-LEAD

A second system is the single-drive, flyer-lead arrangement (Figure 3). The flyer (1) is typically driven from the front, or orifice end (2) by a single drive cord (5). The bobbin (3) is retarded, or braked, by an adjustable friction band (4). This is sometimes called a

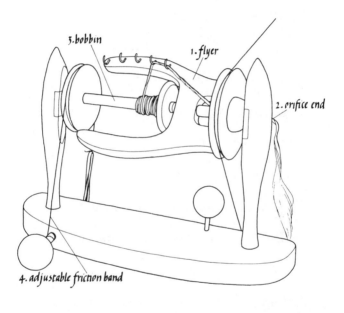

3. bobbin

1. flyer

2. orifice end

4. adjustable friction band

Figure 3. *Single-drive, flyer-lead, or Scotch tension, system.*

"Scotch tension". In this system the bobbin tends to remain at rest, while the flyer rotates. If the spinner holds back on the yarn, the bobbin will be pulled around in step with the flyer. When the spinner introduces slack, the bobbin stalls, being retarded by the friction band. Take-up rate is determined by the degree of braking; the tighter the brake band, the greater the flyer lead, and the greater the take-up.

One variation of this system (Figure 4) is driven from the rear, the side away from the orifice. It looks similar to the double-drive, bobbin-lead arrangement. A single drive cord (1) however, is led over the flyer whorl (2). A brake band (3) is led over the bobbin whorl (4), as above. Any double-drive system can be modified to operate in this fashion.

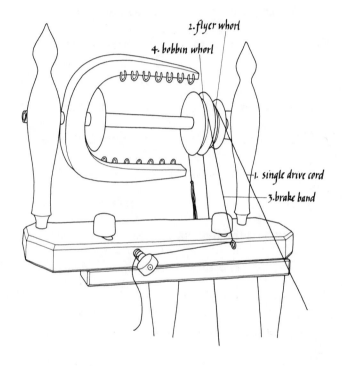

2. flyer whorl

4. bobbin whorl

1. single drive cord

3. brake band

Figure 4. *Single-drive, flyer-lead variation.*

SINGLE-DRIVE, BOBBIN-LEAD

A third arrangement is the single-drive, bobbin-lead system (see Figure 5). In this case, the drive cord (1) is led over the bobbin whorl (2). The bobbin is free to rotate on the flyer shaft. The flyer (3) is indirectly connected to the bobbin (4) by the newly spun yarn (5). As a result of bearing friction, the flyer tends to remain at rest. When the spinner holds back on the yarn, the flyer will rotate in phase with the bobbin. When yarn tension is relaxed, however, the flyer stalls. The net result is bobbin-lead. The degree of lead is adjusted by changing bearing clearance and load. Bearing clearance is changed by clamping or unclamping the leather bearing around the flyer shaft (6). Bearing load is changed by increasing or decreasing drive cord tension. Drive

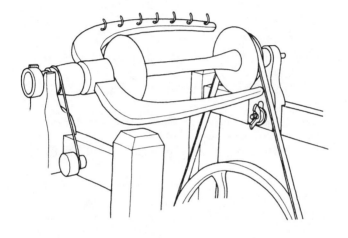

Figure 5. *Single-drive, bobbin-lead system.*

cord tension changes are used to make minor take-up adjustments, while modification of bearing clearance results in gross changes of take-up rate.

SPINDLE

The true spindle is found on some modern and much old equipment (see Figure 6). The basic mechanism consists of a spindle or spike (1) with a permanently attached whorl (2). The spindle disk or cop (3) keeps spun yarn from jamming the bearings (4), and allows more compact build-up during winding-on. A single drive cord (5) is led over the whorl and around the drive wheel. A variation of the basic spindle is found in Figure 7. In this case, an intermediate or accelerating head is used; this arrangement is often called a Minor's

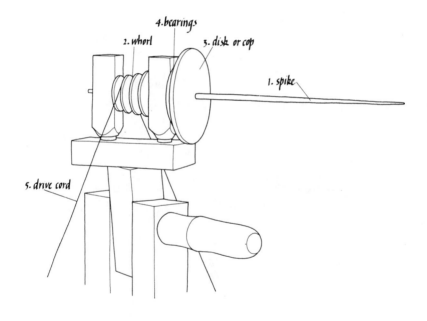

Figure 6. *Spindle, or spike, system.*

head. Spinning on either is much like spin-

ning on a drop spindle, although there is

some difference in technique.

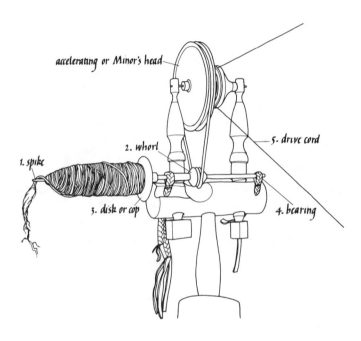

accelerating or Minor's head

2. whorl

1. spike

3. disk or cop

5. drive cord

4. bearing

Figure 7. *A variation of the basic system.*

COMPARISON AND COMMENT

Each spinning mechanism has limiting characteristics. A brief evaluation follows, with both positive and negative values stressed.

Double-drive, bobbin-lead

Positive. Most precise, over a narrow range. Efficient, from the standpoint of energy input vs. yarn output. Can spin fine, low-twist yarn.

Negative. Least flexible. Double drive cord is troublesome. Must take flyer apart to change bobbins. Requires knowledgeable manufacture and repair, as component relationship is critical.

Single-drive, flyer-lead

Positive. Flexible, wide range. Bobbins are easy to change. Component fitting is not critical. A good system to learn with, as it is tolerant of operator error, and has only one simple adjustment.

Negative. Tends to be sensitive to brake adjustments, and frequent adjustment of the brake band may be required. Rear drive version requires flyer disassembly to change bobbins.

Single-drive, bobbin-lead

Positive. Flexible, wide range. Drive ratio is determined by bobbin whorl diameter, and therefore is easily changed. Very efficient, from standpoint of energy input/yarn output ratio. Component relationship is not critical.

Negative. Sensitive to operator technique. Minor change in bearing condition has pronounced effect. Bobbins require frequent internal lubrication. Difficult to spin fine, low-twist yarn. U.S. spinners tend not to be familiar with system, so correct advice on adjustment is rare.

Spindle

Positive. Will spin anything, from thread to rope. Simplest system. Efficient.

Negative. Requires much energy and practice to become proficient. Unsuited to plying. Traditional designs (great wheels) require much working space. All designs are in short supply.

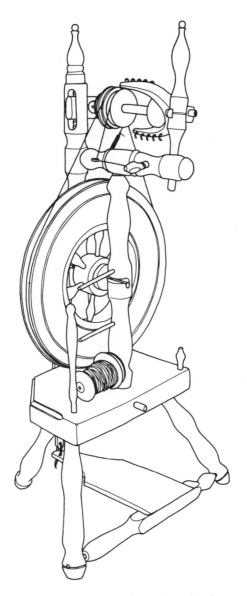

Figure 8. *An upright wheel of traditional style.*

II. WHEEL TYPES

The spinning mechanism is fitted to some type of wheel. Spinning efficiency is essentially a function of drive wheel diameter. Aside from the specific spinning mechanism used, the greater the wheel diameter, the more productive the wheel.

Upright Wheels

For brevity the wheels shown in Figures 8 and 9, and *all* similar arrangements, will be called upright wheels. Such wheels have an advantage in that they require a minimum of working space, and they are portable; a result of the small driving wheel, typically 15 inches

Figure 9. *A newer upright wheel.*

in diameter. The upright illustrated in Figure 9 is an improvement, in that it has a heavy, 19^1/$_2$-inch wheel. It is a good spinner.

SAXON WHEELS

Figure 10 illustrates what will be called a saxon wheel, a style of wheel that is more

Figure 10. *Saxon wheel.*

productive than the uprights. Increased productivity is a result of the larger driving wheel, 22 inches being average. Saxon wheels are obviously less portable than the uprights, although a well-built wheel will readily disassemble.

SPINDLES

Spindle wheels are of many styles, three of which are shown here. Figure 11 illustrates the great or walking wheel, a large, impressive affair. The treadled spike spinner shown in Figure 12 is essentially an upright (see Figures 8, 9) and is a compact, brutally efficient device. The portable spindles shown in Figure 13 are an Indian charkha and "banjo" charkha. They are associated with cotton spinning, and perform well.

Figure 11. *Great, or walking, wheel.*

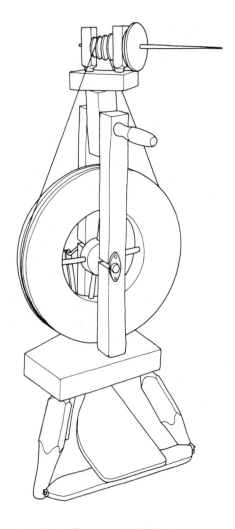

Figure 12. *A spindle-type upright wheel.*

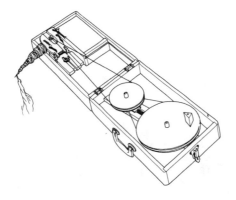

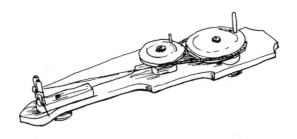

Figure 13. *An Indian "book" charkha (top) and an Amos "banjo" charkha.*

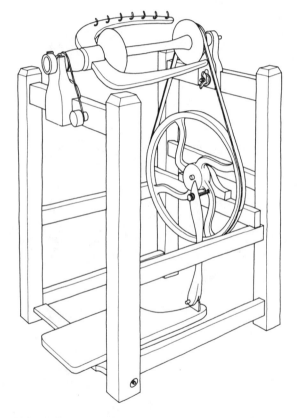

Figure 14. *A bulk spinner.*

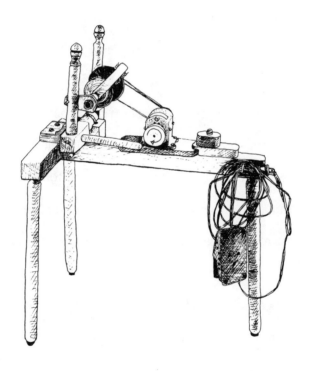

Figure 15. *A motor spinner.*

SPECIAL EQUIPMENT

Several other arrangements are in general use. The bulk spinner (see Figure 14) is designed to produce heavy, bulky yarns. As a class, bulk spinners require a high energy input, and their weight and permanent assembly make them semi-portable. They are essentially a specialized tool. The motorized spinner (Figure 15) is electrically powered. Motor spinners tend to be noisy, and the bobbins are not large. They are good performers, and are useful for plying. Working and storage space requirements are minimal.

This listing is intended to show the prospective spinner a cross-section of available spinning equipment, and does not pretend to be complete.

III. THE IDEAL WHEEL

We will begin by saying that with two billion subjective people in this world, no wheel will fit the definition. Study, testing, and comparison, however, have led the author to the following conclusions:

	Upright	Saxon
Wheel diameter:	15-inch min.	20-inch min.
Drive ratio:	10-to-1	15-to-1
Spinning mechanism:	any, including spindle	any flyer type
Orifice, internal diameter:	3/8 inch	same
Bobbin, inside length:	at least 3"	at least $3^1/_2$"
Bobbin diameter—		
front disk:	2 inches	same
rear disk:	3 inches	same

The following criteria apply to a wheel intended for production spinning of garment-weight yarns (that is, yarns that sett in a firm plain weave at more than 12 EPI):

Wheel type: saxon

Wheel diameter: 24-inch minimum

Spinning mechanism: A or C

Drive ratio: at least 16-to-1

Orifice, inside diameter: at least 3/8 inch

Bobbin length, internal: at least $3^{1}/2$ inches

Bobbin diameter—

front disk: at least 3 inches

rear disk: at least $3^{1}/2$ inches

Extra bobbins: at least 2, included with

wheel

Bobbin rack: yes, included

A word or two about drive ratio is in order.

Drive ratio is the relationship between drive wheel diameter and the leading element whorl diameter (usually the bobbin). To find drive ratio, divide wheel diameter by whorl diameter. Thus, a 22-inch wheel connected to a 2-inch whorl achieves a drive ratio of 11-to-1 (22 ÷ 2 = 11). For each revolution of the drive wheel, the whorl will rotate eleven times. A 22-inch wheel connected to a 1½-inch whorl would be 22 ÷ 1.5, or 14.7-to-1, and so on.

A particular wheel should not be selected on the basis of drive ratio alone. The upright wheel shown in Figure 8 can be modified to achieve a drive ratio of 12-to-1. The modification is not satisfactory, as the drive wheel does not have enough momentum to utilize the higher drive ratio. The upright wheel shown in Figure 9, however, is heavier and larger (19 1/2 -inch diameter as opposed to 15 inches) and is practical to drive ratios as high as 16-to-1. It will help to understand the concept if we think of the drive wheel as a device for storing energy between power impulses. The higher the drive ratio, the faster the available stored energy is used. A heavier wheel stores more energy, at a given speed, than a lighter one.

With a 15-to-1 drive ratio, the flyer/bobbin speed will be 15 times the wheel speed. It is practical to treadle a spinning wheel at 100 revolutions per minute (RPM). At this wheel speed, assuming a 15-to-1 drive ratio, the flyer/bobbin speed will be 15 × 100, or 1500 RPM. Assuming the spinner is producing a yarn with a twist count of ten turns per inch

(TPI), it follows that 150 inches of yarn are produced in one minute (IPM). To find yarn production in IPM, divide flyer/bobbin speed (in RPM) by the twist count (in TPI) of the desired yarn. Thus, a flyer/bobbin speed of 1000 RPM and a twist count of 20 TPI will result in theoretical production of 50 IPM. Actual production is always less, due to slippage. A properly adjusted system will achieve 80% of theoretical production, all other factors remaining equal. Low drive ratios slip less than high ones; a 6-to-1 realizing 95% of theoretical, a 28-to-1, correctly adjusted, no less than 80%.

The treadle is an area often overlooked. The effective treadle length is important, as it affects both operator comfort and wheel efficiency. A suitable treadle will have an effec-

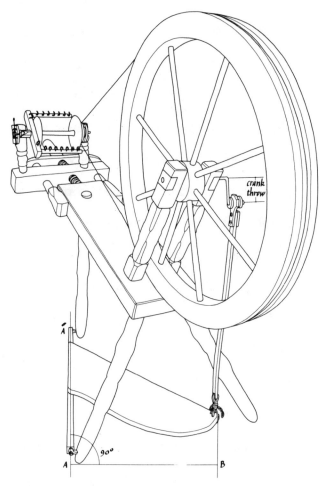

Figure 16. *Treadle should be six times the length of the crank throw.*

tive length (Figure 16) of at least six times the crank throw. Effective treadle length is measured at right angles to the treadle pivot axis (A, Á), and is measured from the footman attaching point (B) to the pivot line. Thus, a wheel with a two-inch crank throw requires an effective treadle length of 12 inches.

A spinning wheel used in production work is large, and of durable, robust construction. If the wheel is built of wood, the following timbers are suitable, and are listed in no particular order:

- Sugar maple (*Acer saccharum*)
- Black cherry (*Prunus serotina*)
- Beech (*Fagus grandifolia*)
- Sweet birch (*Betula lenta*)
- White oak (*Quercus alba*)

- Red oak (*Quercus rubra*, and others)
- White ash (*Fraxinus americana*, and others)
- Black walnut (*Juglans nigra*)

Other timbers are suitable, as long as the requirements of strength, weight, durability, and economic availability are satisfied. It is not wise to assume that the finish on the wheel accurately represents the timber used in construction.

In closing, we offer a few words of advice: Do not equate performance with price, or a spiffy appearance. Do not expect the wheel to do something that you, or it, cannot do. Try to spin on the wheel before you buy; most dealers and makers will allow this. Learn to spin, as it gives you a frame of reference. No one should buy a car without first learning to

drive and taking a test ride. It is the same with
spinning wheels.

"Spin ye now
of the good brown flax
and in the spinning
rejoyce"
... *inscription on 18th-century flax wheel*

APPENDIX A

DRIVE RATIOS

This table illustrates the nominal drive ratios obtained with specific wheel and whorl diameters. The inclusion of letters indicates the general suitability of that combination for a particular fiber.

Using a 22-inch wheel as an example, we find that a whorl diameter of $1\,^1/_2$ inches will give us a drive ratio of 14.7-to-1, and that the combination is suitable for general wool spinning. Note that a 26-inch wheel is able to use a higher drive ratio ($1\,^1/_2$" whorl, 17.3-to-1) for general wool spinning, as the greater drive wheel diameter makes the use of higher ratios a practicality (see Section III, "The Ideal Wheel").

Whorl Diameter

	Wheel Diameter							
	14"	16"	18"	20"	22"	24"	26"	28"
5/8"	22.4	25.6	28.8	32	35.2	38.4	41.6	44.8
3/4"	18.7	21.3	24	26.7	29.3	32	34.7	37.3
7/8"	16	18.2	10.6	22.8	25.1	27.4	29.7	32
1"	14	16C	18C	20C	22C	24C	26	28
1 1/8"	12.4C	14.2SS	16SS	17.8	19.5	21.3SS	23.1C	24.9
1 1/4"	11.2	12.8	14.4	16SS	17.6SS	19.2	20.8SS	22.4C
1 3/8"	10.2SS	11.6	13.1	14.5	16	17.4	18.9	20.4SS
1 1/2"	9.3	10.7W	12W	13.3W	14.7W	16W	17.3W	18.7
1 5/8"	8.6W	9.8	11.1	12.3	13.5	14.8	16	17.2W
1 3/4"	8	9.1L	10.3L	11.4	12.6	13.7L	14.9L	16
1 7/8"	7.5L	8.5	9.6	10.7L	11.7L	12.8	13.9	14.9L
2"	7	8S	9S	10	11	12S	13S	14S
2 1/4"	6.2S	7.1	8	8.9S	9.8S	10.7	11.6	12.4
2 1/2"	5.6	6.4	7.2	8	8.8	9.6	10.4	11.2
2 3/4"	5.1	5.8	6.5	7.3	8	8.7	9.4	10.2
3"	4.7	5.3	6	6.7	7.3	8	8.7	9.3

W = wool   L = line flax (linen)   C = cotton   S = silk   SS = silk, short staple (noil) and other short-staple fibers

APPENDIX B

USEFUL TRIVIA

1. Grease-spun yarn may lose 40% of its weight during scouring.

2. Most plying is done between one and four turns per inch (TPI). *

3. Wheel efficiency may drop 50% when plying heavy yarns.

4. A beginning to intermediate spinner should produce 150 yards of six TPI yarn per hour.

5. An intermediate to advanced spinner will do 250 yards of six TPI yarn per hour.

6. An advanced spinner will produce 350 yards of six TPI yarn per hour.

7. A production spinner should produce 500 yards of six TPI yarn per hour, or should enter some other field of endeavor.

8. A spinning wheel with a drive ratio of 10-to-1 is capable of producing 240 yards of six TPI yarn per hour (treadled at 120 RPM).

9. A wheel with a 20-to-1 drive ratio can produce 450 yards of six TPI yarn per hour (treadled at 120 RPM).

10. A wheel with a 30-to-1 drive ratio is capable of producing over 700 yards of six TPI yarn per hour (treadled at 120 RPM).

APPENDIX C

CAUTIONS

1. Keep a spare drive cord taped under the wheel table.

2. Remember to oil well, including inside bobbins. Use heavy (drugstore) mineral oil.

3. When spinning raw wool, the flyer, orifice, and hooks will gum up. Clean with cotton swabs and rubbing alcohol.

4. Place wheel on a carpet, or use rubber feet (or crutch tips) to stop skidding.

5. To finish a kit wheel, we use oil such as Watco®. Leave wheel groove rough.

6. Do not use wax or furniture polish on wheel groove or whorls (see No. 7, below).

7. A slipping drive cord may be helped by applying beeswax.

8. Drive cords are best made of soft cotton twine, such as eight- or ten-ply package string. Splicing or sewing ends together is preferred, although a knot like the fishermen's bend will serve well. Big, hard knots are out.

9. Heavy oil or light grease should be used on wheel bearings. Do not use pencil lead or graphite.

10. Remember to move the yarn from hook to hook as spinning proceeds, to fill the bobbin evenly. This makes quite a difference when reeling off the loaded bobbins.

APPENDIX D

QUESTIONS & ANSWERS

The following is excerpted from 101 Questions for Spinners, *(Straw Into Gold, 1978). Responses signed A.A. are by Alden Amos; S.D. is Susan Druding. Reprinted with permission of Susan Druding for Straw Into Gold.*

I want to spin my own yarn from our Dorset sheep's wool. What is the best wheel to buy?

I recommend that you not buy until you have *tried* a number of different wheels. Perhaps you can borrow a friend's wheel, or attend a local spinning demonstration. Spinning classes are a good way to share various wheels, and many spinning and weaving stores rent wheels by the week or month. In any case, learn to spin first.

—*A.A.*

It is very hard to tell anyone what the "best" wheel for them is. Do you already know how to spin on a wheel? You should definitely learn how before purchasing a wheel. I usually suggest that students start out with one of the inexpensive "kit" wheels (imported or domestic). You can always sell it (assembled and stained) for at least what you paid when you are ready to trade up to a better wheel.

—*S.D.*

My Ashford wheel makes a clunking sound when I pedal it. How do I fix it?

The Ashford drive wheel is secured on the wheel crank by a slip-in cross pin. Generally the clunk is caused by the pin's being a loose fit through the crankshaft. This allows the crank to "flop" a few degrees as the treadle passes its highest point. The indicated repair is to refit with a larger (tighter) pin. If the condition is allowed to continue, the hole through the wooden hub will become battered and enlarged, which will require that both hub and axle be redrilled and a new pin installed.

—A.A.

The most common cause is that the footman and treadle may not be snug against each other. If the fastening is a leather tie, snug it up. You need to figure out for sure where your particular clunk is before you can fix it. Have a friend treadle while you crawl around the wheel to listen.

—S.D.

How can I make my old Ashford wheel spin faster? I have read that there is a "speed kit" available. How does it work? Will it hurt the finish to put it on?

Since about 1978, a "speed" whorl has been standard on Ashford wheels. The "speed kit" you refer to was designed for older models to improve the drive ratio; it consists of a supplementary small drive whorl that mounts in front of the standard whorl. The Ashford kit does require two screw holes in the front face of the standard flyer. The typical standard Ashford comes from the box with a drive ratio of about 7:1 (one turn of the drive wheel gives seven turns to the flyer). The kit will improve the ratio to something like 10:1 or 12:1, so that one turn of the drive wheel will result in ten or twelve turns of the flyer.

—*A.A.*

What should I use to oil my antique spinning wheel?

Assuming that you mean lubrication, a good, heavy, clear mineral oil (available at the drugstore) will give excellent service. Sewing-machine oil, 3-in-1 Oil, and the like are too light for hardworking wheels. In our shop we use both mineral oil and light grease. 30-weight motor oil does very well, although some people do not like the smell. If you are talking about improving the appearance of the wood by using oil, I pass, as the refinishing of antiques is a complicated field.

—*A.A.*

If you mean to oil the moving parts: mineral oil. If you mean the wood surfaces: paste wax.

—*S.D.*

What is the best thing to use for driving bands?

The ideal drive band or cord would be limp, rough, nonelastic, uniform in thickness with no seam or join, easily and quickly installed, adjustable in length, and cheap. We have yet to find it. For practical purposes, many things will give satisfactory results. We generally use an eight- or ten-ply soft cotton twine, joined with a fisherman's bend. When it gets frazzled and raggedy, or too long (it *will* wear out!), take five minutes and put a new one on. Most spinning/weaving shops carry suitable cords and twines.

—A.A.

Use a soft, thick cotton twine (such as packages are tied with), as a hard, smooth cord will slip too much and lose friction. Keep a spare cord taped under the wheel's table for emergency repairs. I tie a tight, hard square knot despite all the advice about splicing—but then I am not a terribly good splicer!

—S.D.

My drive band keeps jumping off, even though I tighten the tension. The wheel isn't warped or bent. What do you think is the problem?

Several possibilities on this. Most frequent is misalignment between flyer assembly and drive wheel. Another common problem is the drive band itself—it could be too bulky for the grooves. Again, in the case of double drive, the drive cord crossing may be reversed for the direction in which you wish to spin. There are other reasons for it, but judging from your picture I will say that the long loose ends on your drive cord are the culprits.

—A.A.

You may have too large a knot in the belt. You may be turning the wheel with your hand on the rim and knocking it off. The alignment of your flyer pulley may be off with respect to the wheel. Stand next to your wheel and sight along the groove in the drive wheel to the drive pulleys. If they are out of line, adjust accordingly. Sometimes it is just a maiden that turns out of line as you are spinning, or it may need a real move of the maidens. Once you figure out what is out of line, you can figure out what to fix.

—S.D.

My wheel won't take up the yarn fast enough. Are there any adjustments besides the tension for this?

If you are using a single-drive, flyer-lead wheel such as the Ashford, take-up can be increased by adjusting the brake band on the bobbin. If it is a single-drive, bobbin-lead arrangement, there is usually an adjustment to retard the flyer. A double-drive wheel often has two grooves (or more) on the flyer whorl, and maximum take-up is realized by using the smallest diameter groove on the *bobbin* whorl and the largest diameter groove on the *flyer* whorl. Generally speaking, any further take-up will have to be arranged by having the flyer and bobbin modified by a wheel maker.

—A.A.

If you have a double-drive wheel and increase the difference in the flyer and bobbin whorl diameters, the wheel will draw in faster (e.g., turn down the diameter of the bobbin whorl); this will also make the wheel spin faster. Be sure to oil the bobbins inside and the maidens so everything turns smoothly.

—S.D.

I have an old flax wheel in perfect condition. Can I use it to spin wool?

Yes, you can. Flax wheels, however, are set up to do a specific job (i.e., spin linen) and have small orifices, small hooks, and a relatively high drive ratio/low take-up. As a result, the wheel will be efficient with wool only when you are spinning a fine yarn. This will limit the wools that you can use, as best results will require long staples (Lincoln fleece, for example).

—A.A.

Certainly, but fine wool yarns only. Flax wheels were set up to spin very fine linen yarns and will spin wool to this diameter also. Often they have very tiny bobbins and small hooks—you might want to have a whole new flyer assembly and bobbins made if yours are uncomfortably small.

—S.D.

I want to spin a heavy yarn for tapestries and rugs. What is the best wheel?

A "heavy" tapestry yarn typically measures between 50 and 200 yards per pound. Such a yarn can be produced on the various bulk spinners, such as the California, Indian Valley, or the Ashford Indian Spinner. Where the spinner's skill and speed allow it, I recommend a treadled, upright spike wheel. And frankly, I think an electric drill with a big hook inserted into the chuck does a fine job for really bulky yarns.

—A.A.

Depends what you mean by "heavy". If you want it as fat and funky and big in diameter as your thumb, you probably want a bulk spinner or a spike wheel. Or you may use a Navajo spindle. If you mean a medium weight such as knitting worsted, you should be able to do it on most contemporary wheels. I do not use enough of the really fat yarn in my weaving that it is worth my having a special bulk spinning wheel, so I use a Navajo spindle and find that it is quite fast. (And there are none of the frustrations of trying to get the fat yarn to draw into the orifice and over the hooks of a bulk spinner. I do use a spike wheel to twist heavy yarn from wool top. I find I can twist a pound of top into a smooth, heavy yarn in about two minutes!)

—*S.D.*

I travel a lot and like to spin when we are camping. What is a good wheel for that?

Personally, I would not take a wheel on a camping trip, and the only time I travel with one is when I am transporting it from shop to customer or to spinning demonstrations, lectures, and the like. If an overpowering urge to spin comes upon me, I dig around in my pack and come up with my heavy-duty bobbin winder, or improvise a drop spindle.

—*A.A.*

Depends on how you travel and where. If you are "car camping", a charkha wheel might be fun (it folds up into an attaché case–sized box). If you are hiking or backpacking, take along a light drop spindle and lightweight fibers.

—*S.D.*

I have heard that the Shakers made the best spinning wheels ever. Is that true?

The Shaker wheel makers were conscientious workmen who used carefully selected materials in well-thought-out ways, taking their time and using proven techniques. So did a lot of other (non-Shaker) wheel makers.

—A.A.

All their products were well made and functional, but I would not say they were the best wheel makers. The Canadian wool wheel (see the Pennington book listed in the bibliography) is extremely functional and suited to its purpose. Any wheel specially made for a certain use which worked well could be called "best" in its own category.

—S.D.

What is the difference between the types of castle wheels? Between a Brunswick and a Saxony?

Nothing or everything. Around our shop, Castle, with a capital "C", means an Irish Castle wheel, a tableless tripod arrangement with the drive wheel *above* the flyer, and a small "c" denotes a conventional small upright, with a single small table, the wheel just above the table, and the flyer either left above, right above, or centered over the wheel.

Saxony and Brunswick are more or less the same thing, though we call the larger wheels Saxonies and the smaller, Brunswicks. A Saxony/Brunswick wheel has a single tilted table with the drive wheel mounted at the lower end of the table and the flyer and bobbin at the opposite and upper end.

—A.A.

My old great wheel has what my father calls a miner's head. Can you tell me anything about it?

A miner's head (or Minor's head, named after Amos Minor) is an accelerating device much used on great wheels (see page 16). Technically, all Minor's heads are accelerated spindles, although all accelerated spindles are not Minor's heads. (This is because his design was ripped off rather early on.) The operation of the Minor's head is simple and ingenious. Power from the great driving wheel is routed to a primary whorl, which is attached to a larger secondary whorl. A separate drive band is routed from the secondary whorl over the spindle whorl proper, giving overall wheel-to-spindle drive ratios of approximately 250:1. Amos Minor invented and perfected his Minor's head in the early 1800s (1803 is given by one source, and the device and its copies were marketed until at least the Civil War era. New "Minor's " heads are available today.

—A.A.

I saw a demonstration where the spinner put a pencil into the orifice of her spinning wheel and then spun a thick yarn onto the pencil. Is there a special wheel to do this sort of spinning?

Yes, there áre several: the Rio Grande, the Penguin quill, and the Amos treadle spike, to name a few.

—A.A.

Yes, there are a couple of types of wheel which spin from a spindle or "spike". These wheels are versatile—no orifice or hooks means you may spin odd textures and thicknesses without getting hung up. Among their primary advantages are their simplicity and their efficiency—the large number of twists per treadle. The fast spike wheels require some skill to use. Very fine yarns may also be spun on them (similarly to the great wheel), as there is no flyer causing a pull on the yarn being spun. However, when the cop reaches a large diameter, a fine yarn can easily break, burying the end beyond reclamation.

—S.D.

My driving band slips after it has been on the wheel for a short time. Should I use something on it to make it sticky? I don't want to hurt the finish.

Slipping drive bands are the result of several things, and it would be best to check each. First, be sure that the cord is suitable (see page 43). Next, don't forget that most drive bands stretch throughout their usable life, and the tension will have to be readjusted as needed. Third, check to see that the knot, splice, sewing, or whatever you use to join the ends of the drive cord is not slipping. Fourth, be sure that the tension adjustment is positive in action and stays where you set it.

Last, check that the wheel and whorl grooves are not loaded with oil, wax, and junk. If all of the above are in good order, then try a little pure beeswax rubbed into the cord. A commercial belt dressing will work just as well, or better.

—A.A.

Try a little beeswax. You may wish to switch to a softer, thicker cotton drive cord. Be careful not to get oil on it while you are oiling your wheel.

—S.D.

I am going to Sweden to study weaving for a year. Do I need to do anything special to my wheel for storage?

I'd recommend that the wheel be stored as follows: Loosen all tension devices; remove all yarn from bobbins; clean orifice, hooks, and bearings; reapply fresh lubricant to bearing surfaces; store the wheel in a cool, dry place, out of reach of the sun, the rain, pets, curious children, and experimenters. Do not stack or pile anything on the wheel, or lean or rest anything against it. Leave the wheel in its upright or spinning position. The room or place in which the wheel is stored should also be comfortable (not too hot, cold, dry, wet, etc.) for humans.

—A.A.

Don't leave it where the sun will beat on it or where a furnace or heater will blast it with hot air. If you live in the country and there will be no heat in a cold, damp house, you might want to store it with friends who will be home. Best not to leave it in a garage, attic, or basement if it will get damp.

—S.D.

The legs fall out of my spinning wheel whenever it is moved. Should I glue them in place?

You can glue them, although it is not a good idea. Most wheels, both old and new, are designed to come apart. This can be a valuable feature. The best plan to solve the falling-out problem is to stuff a little bit of greasy wool around the legs before putting them in place. Of course, if your wheel is of a type that does not have friction-fitted legs, then it is another thing entirely. Some old wheels had the legs held in place by wedges or cross-pins, and many new wheels require the use of metal pins, screws, and the like. A few are permanently installed. In any case, find out what the builder's intentions were before making any drastic changes in the assembly routine.

—A.A.

What is a good wax or polish to use? I keep feeling I should put *something* on my spinning wheel and loom.

In our shop we use both penetrating/sealing oils and wax for assembled kit wheels and for our own products. For a finished wheel, one that has been stained and sealed, for example, we recommend the judicious and sparse application of a good paste wax. We do not recommend the use of spray waxes, water-based waxes, the various ingenious furniture polishes, etc.

—A.A.

I don't bother with them, but I have had friends recommend regular furniture paste wax.

—S.D.

How big a yarn should I be able to spin on my wheel? The orifice is 1/2 inch in diameter. I do well spinning fine yarns, but can't do really fat ones.

A very good question. In my opinion, the orifice of a flyer and the muzzle of a shotgun have much in common—they impress the hell out of whomever they are pointed at. Forget shotgun muzzles. The bigness of the yarn that can be spun on a given wheel/flyer combination is dependent on several factors besides orifice diameter. The drive ratio, the take-up ratio, the flyer/hook arrangement, the size of the bobbin, diameter and weight of the driving wheel, the geometry of the wheel—all of these play a part. In short, a large orifice alone does not a thick yarn make. A good, rough rule of thumb to apply is that the orifice should be three times as large as the heaviest yarn to be spun, so a 1/2-inch orifice will allow you to spin a yarn about 3/16 inch in diameter. It is perfectly possible to spin larger yarns, although trying to get a 1/4- or 3/8-inch-thick yarn to feed smoothly and quickly through a 1/2-inch orifice can be an exercise in futility.

—A.A.

Do not believe that just because you have a large orifice on your wheel, you will easily be able to spin fat yarns. Heavy yarns are definitely harder to spin than fine ones. The main reason it is hard to spin heavy yarns is that a little twist goes a long way with them. You need only one turn per inch (or less) for thick yarns; adding more will cause them to be overspun, and you'll then have real problems getting the yarn to wind on over the hooks. The other problem will be your wheel itself. No matter how large the orifice is, if the wheel is not heavy enough to have the power to spin and draw extraheavy yarn in and wind it on, you will have a frustrating time. Most people who want to spin a lot of yarn which is very bulky use a different wheel, called a "bulk spinner" or a spike wheel. I usually use a Navajo spinner for mine.

—*S.D.*

I have a lot of trouble with overspinning. Everything is fine until I get the bobbin about half full; then the overspinning starts. Am I spinning too slowly?

Assuming you are using a double-drive, bobbin-lead wheel, the answer is no, you are not spinning too slowly. The problem you are dealing with is a mechanical characteristic of double-drive wheels caused by the increase in bobbin shaft diameter. As the bobbin fills, it tries to wind on more yarn per revolution relative to the flyer. In theory, this would increase wind-on rate, thereby causing an *under*spun condition. In practice, the opposite occurs. What happens is that the drive band begins to slip on the bobbin whorl. Since take-up rate is determined by the differential speed of the two elements (bobbin and flyer), any slippage on the bobbin whorl results in a considerable reduction in the difference between the two, thereby decreasing take-up rate, and doing so faster than the filling bobbin increases it. The net result of all this is that take-up rate decreases as the bobbin fills. Standard correction for this is to increase drive band tension, thereby reducing whorl slippage. Around here we refer to the problem as the "winch effect". It is not a problem with most single-drive wheels, as the differential speed is not affected by whorl slippage.

—*A.A.*

SELECTED BIBLIOGRAPHY

Anderson, B. *Creative Spinning, Weaving, and Plant Dyeing*. Arco, n.d.

Anderson, Enid. *Encyclopedia of Spinning*.

Born, W. *Ciba Review*, #28, December, 1989.

Davenport, Elsie. *Your Handspinning*. Unicorn.

Druding, Susan. *Notes on Spinning of Bast Fibers*. Straw Into Gold.

Duncan, Molly. *Spin, Dye, and Weave Your Own Wool*. Sterling, 1973.

Fannin, Allen. *Handspinning, Art and Technique*. Van Nostrand Reinhold, 1981.

Hochberg, Bette. *Handspinner's Handbook*. Self-published, 1980. Distributed by Straw Into Gold.

Hoppe, E., and R. Edberg *Carding, Spinning, Dyeing*. Van Nostrand Reinhold, n.d.

Kluger, Marilyn. *The Joy of Spinning*. Simon & Schuster, 1971.

Pennington, David, and Michael Taylor. *A Pictorial Guide to American Spinning Wheels*. Shaker Press.

Raven, Lee. *Hands On Spinning*. Interweave Press, 1987.

Ross, Mabel. *The Encyclopedia of Handspinning*. Interweave Press, 1988.

Svinicki, E. *Step By Step Spinning and Dyeing*. Golden Press, n.d.

Teal, Peter. *Hand Woolcombing and Spinning: A Guide to Worsted From the Spinning Wheel*. Sterling, n.d.

Thompson, G. *Spinning Wheels. The John Horner Collection*. Ulster Museum.